THE ROLLING STONES
BASS COLLECTION

Transcribed by STEVE GORENBERG

Cover photo by Jeffrey Mayer

ISBN 0-7935-8848-0

7777 W. BLUEMOUND RD. P.O. BOX 13819 MILWAUKEE, WI 53213

For all works contained herein:
Unauthorized copying, arranging, adapting, recording or public performance is an infringement of copyright.
Infringers are liable under the law.

Visit Hal Leonard Online at
www.halleonard.com

CONTENTS

4 ANGIE

10 BEAST OF BURDEN

17 DOO DOO DOO DOO DOO (HEARTBREAKER)

23 EMOTIONAL RESCUE

33 HANG FIRE

39 THE HARLEM SHUFFLE

45 IT'S ONLY ROCK 'N' ROLL (BUT I LIKE IT)

56 MISS YOU

65 RESPECTABLE

72 SHE'S SO COLD

80 START ME UP

87 TUMBLING DICE

94 Bass Notation Legend

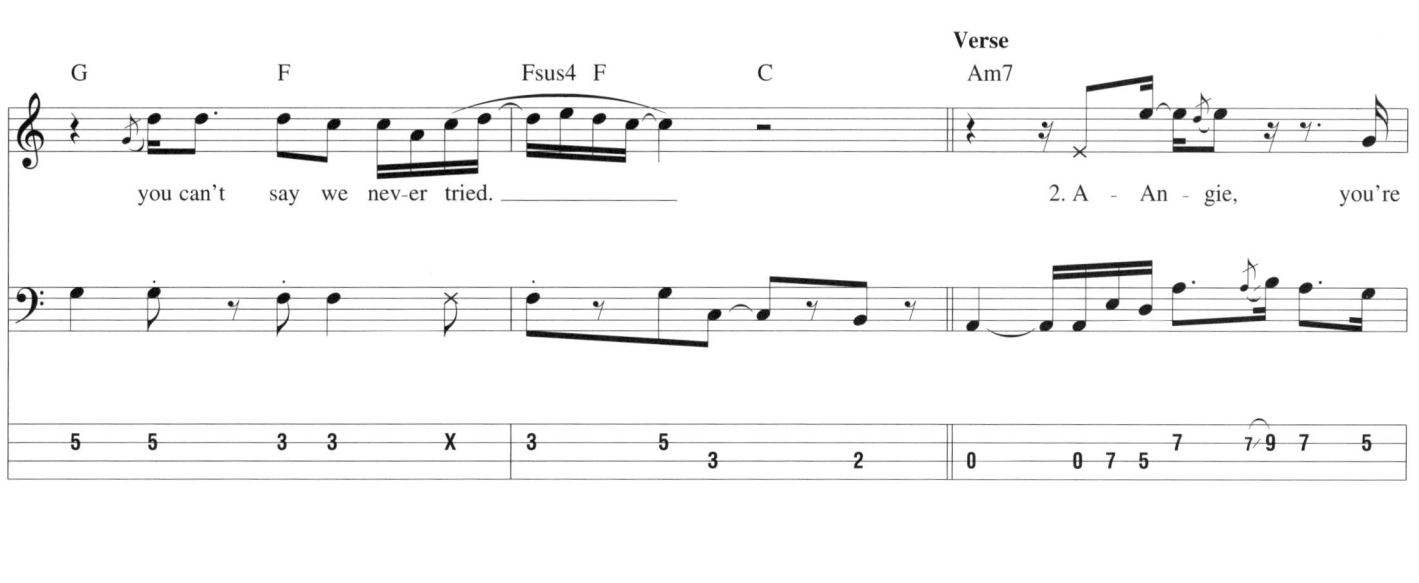
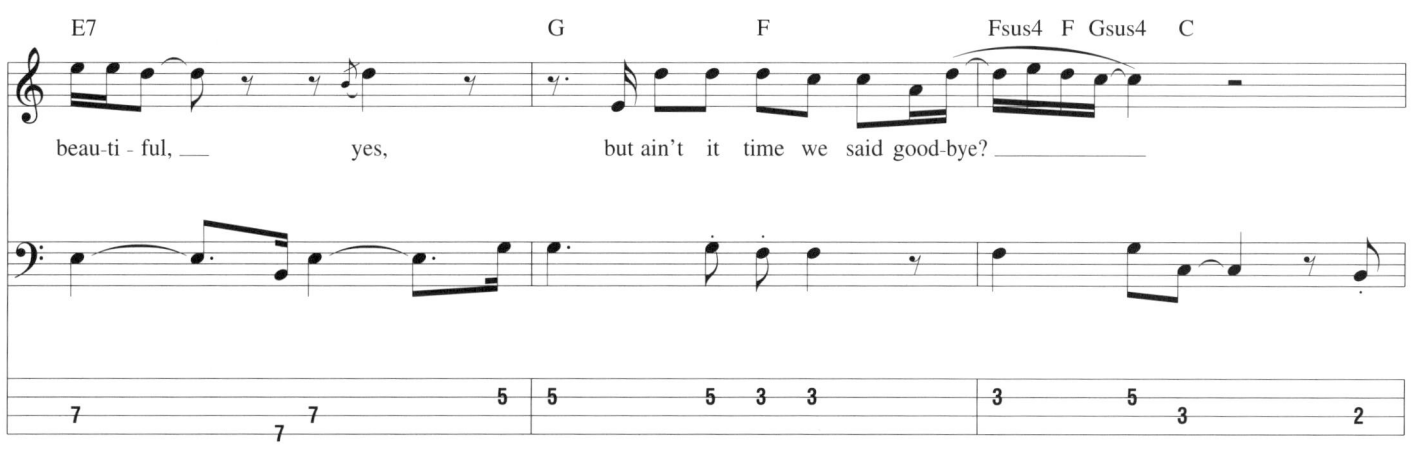

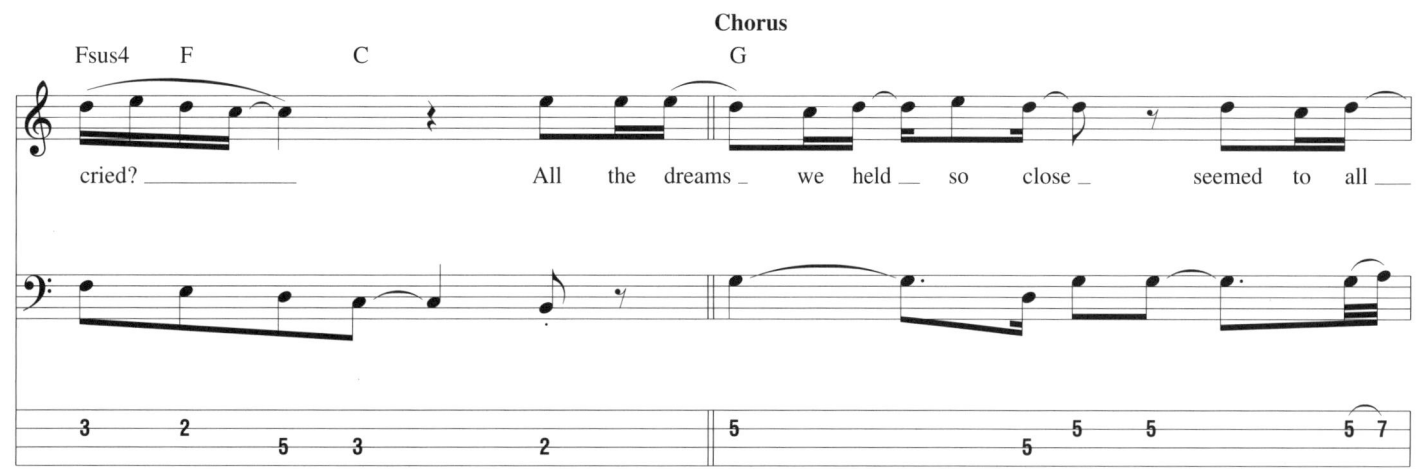

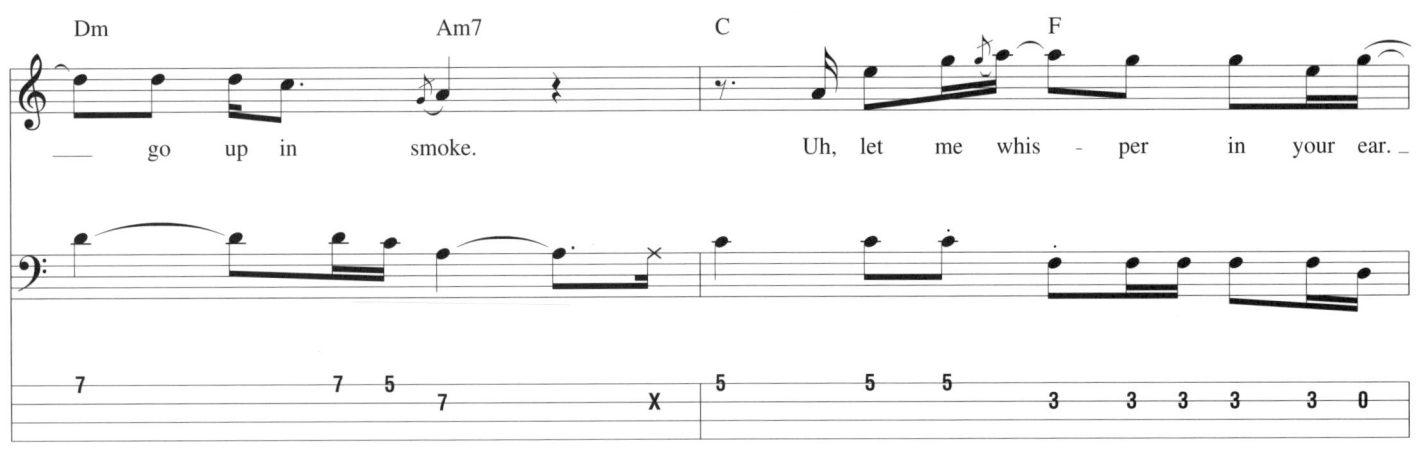
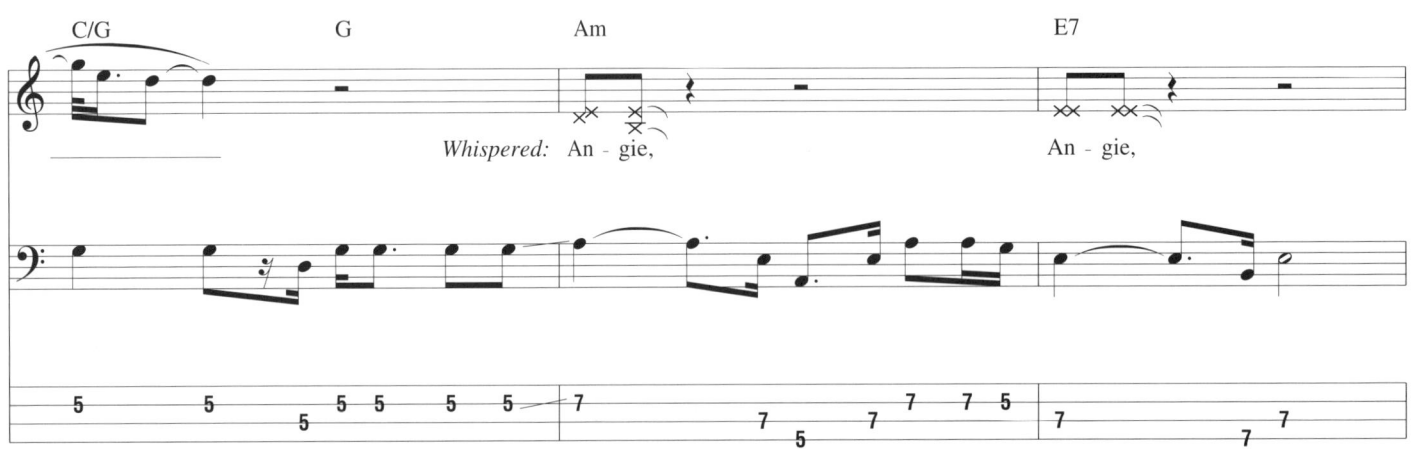
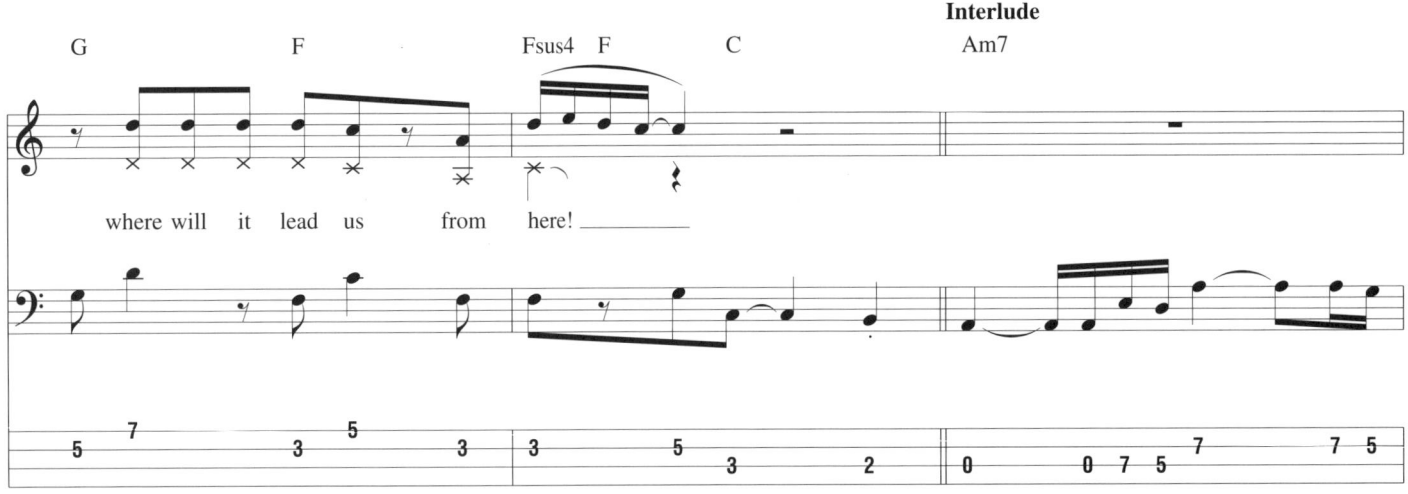
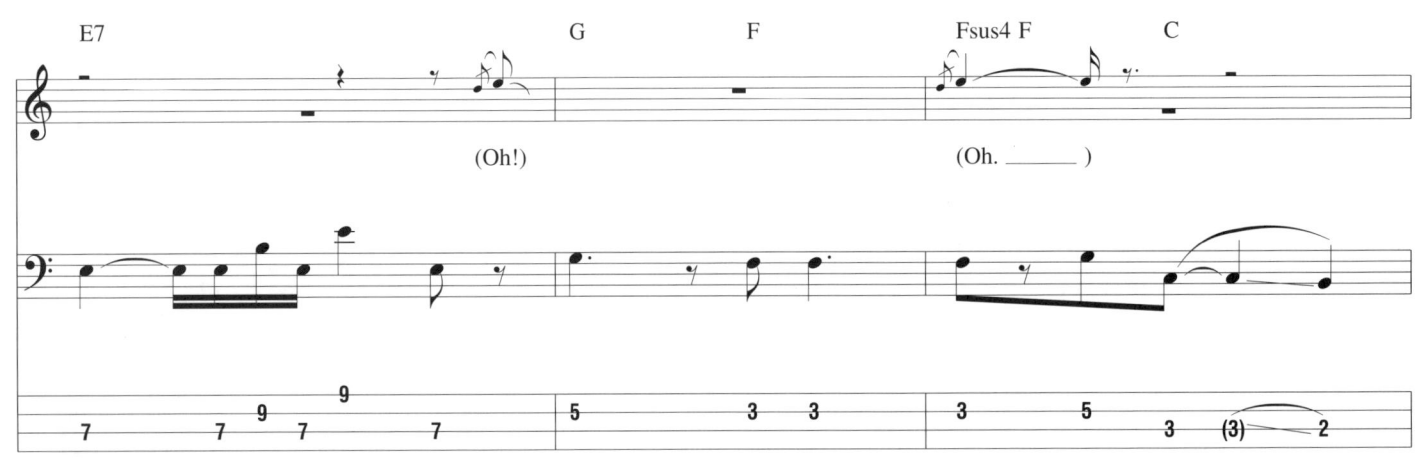

Oh, An-gie don't you weep, all your kis-ses still taste sweet.
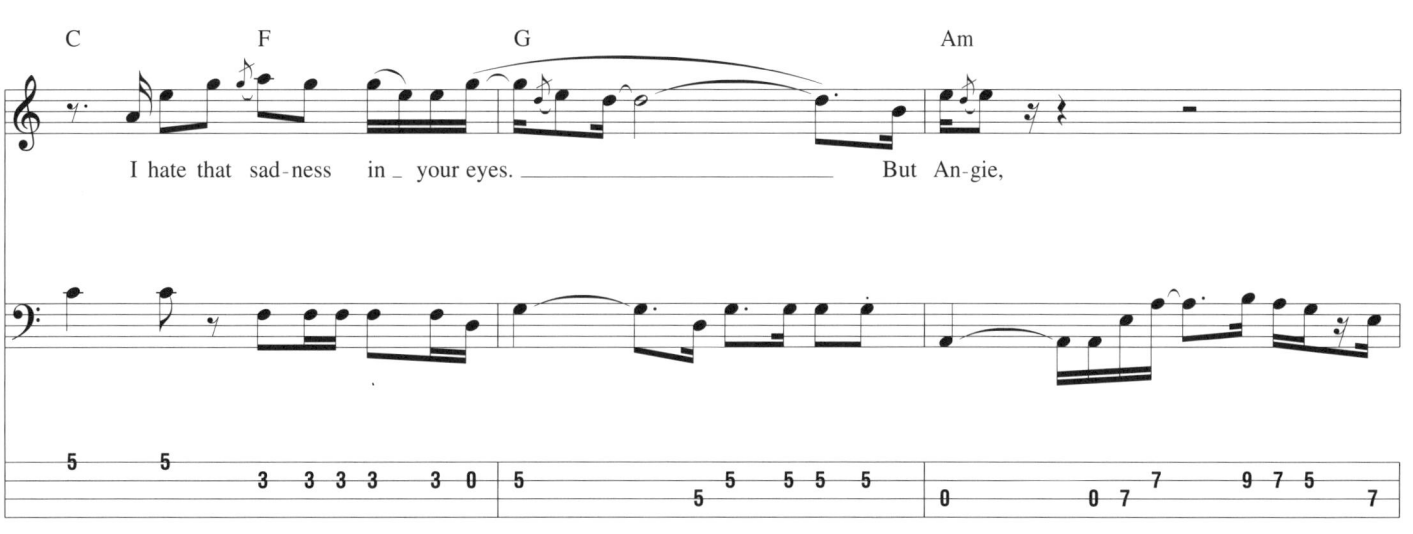
I hate that sad-ness in your eyes. But An-gie,
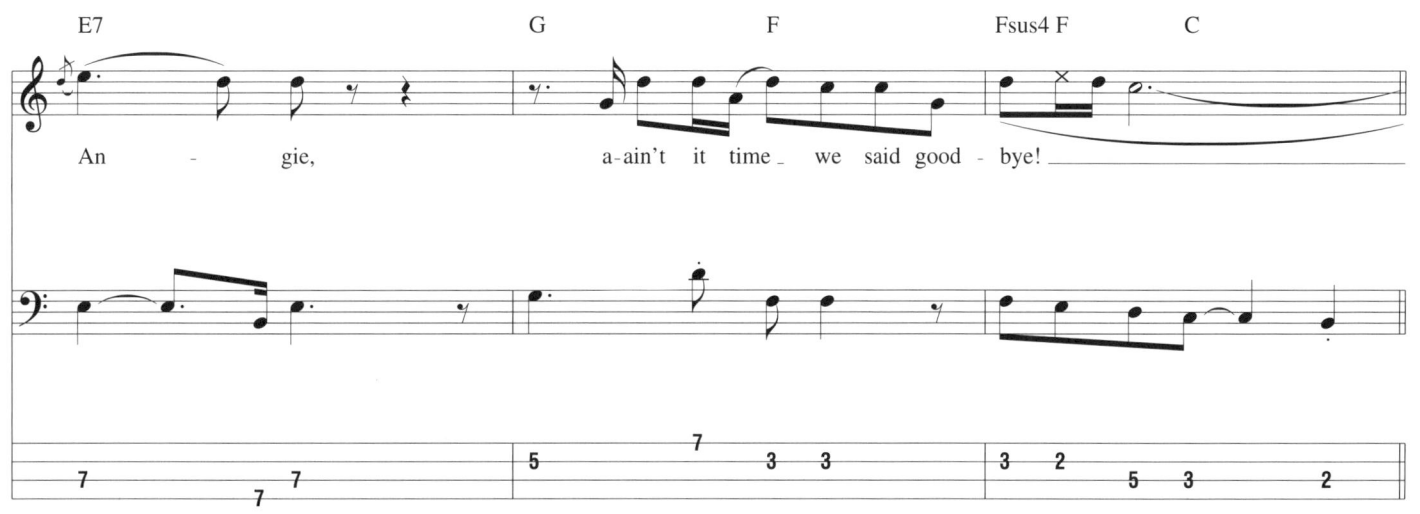
An - gie, a-ain't it time we said good-bye!

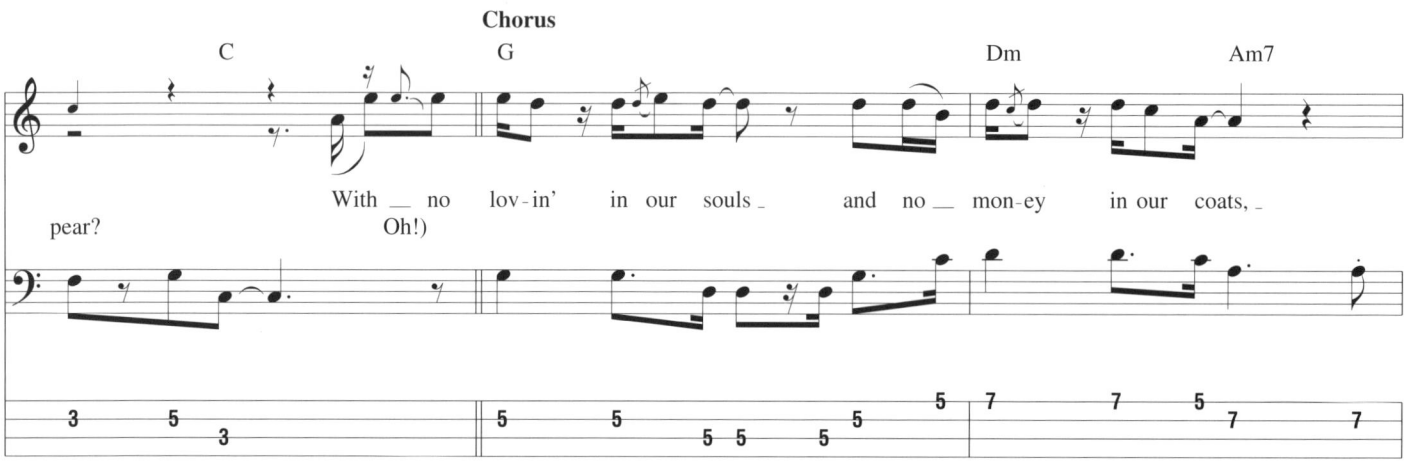
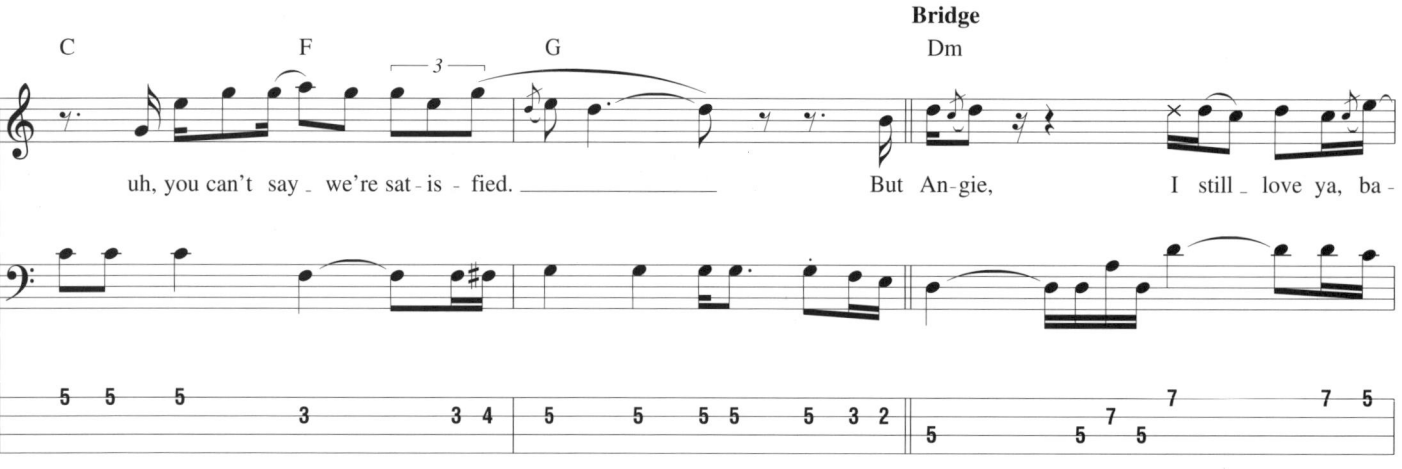
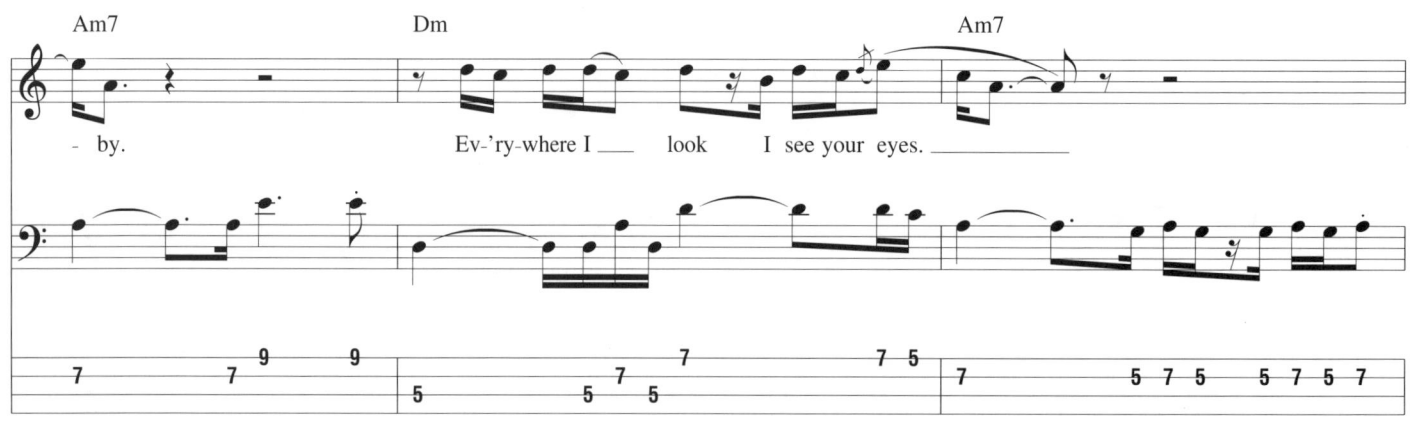

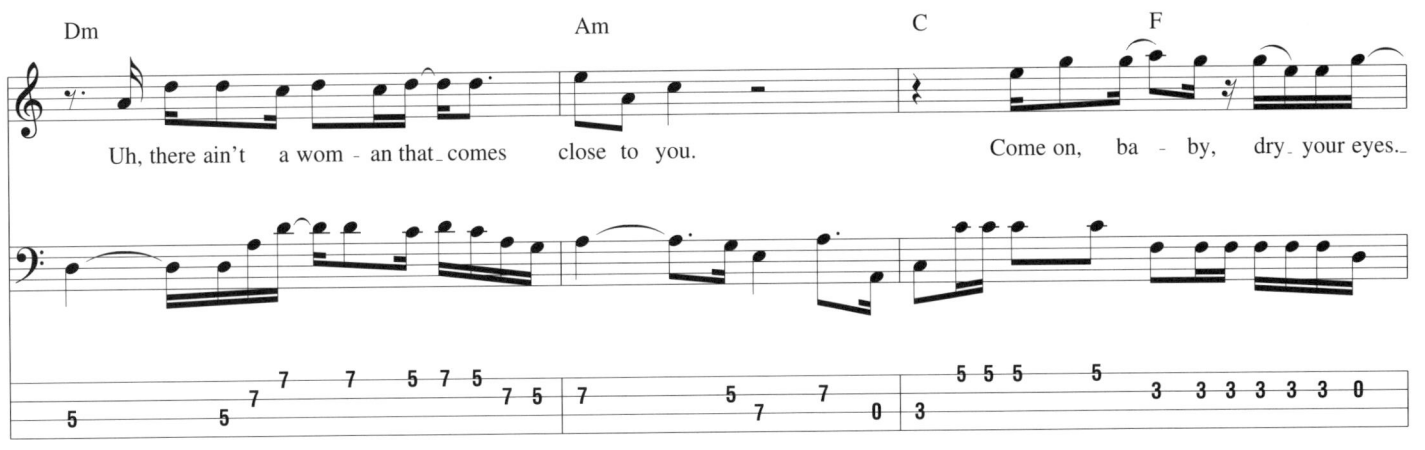

from Some Girls
Beast of Burden
Words and Music by Mick Jagger and Keith Richards

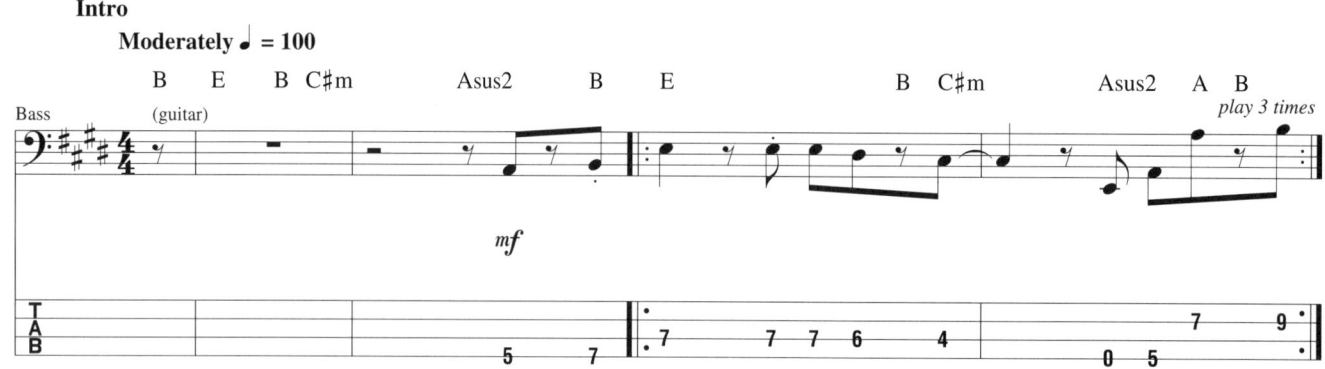

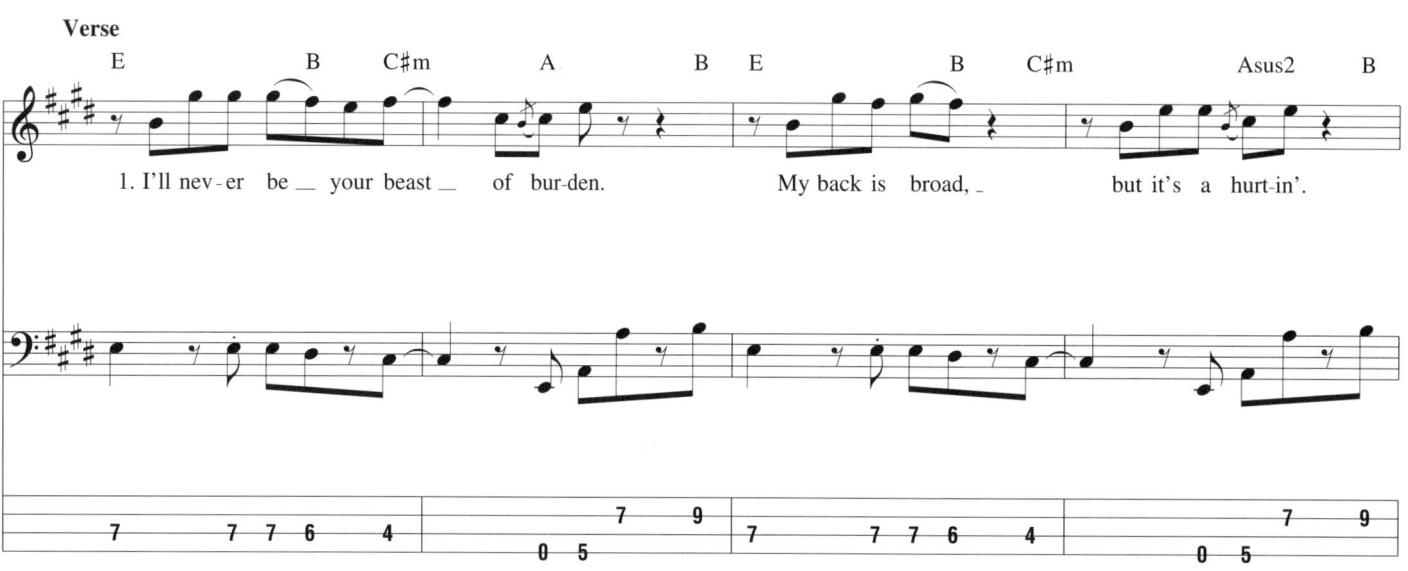

© 1978 EMI MUSIC PUBLISHING LTD.
All Rights for the U.S. and Canada Controlled and Administered by COLGEMS-EMI MUSIC INC.
All Rights Reserved   International Copyright Secured   Used by Permission

from *Goats Head Soup*

Doo Doo Doo Doo Doo
(Heartbreaker)

Words and Music by Mick Jagger and Keith Richards

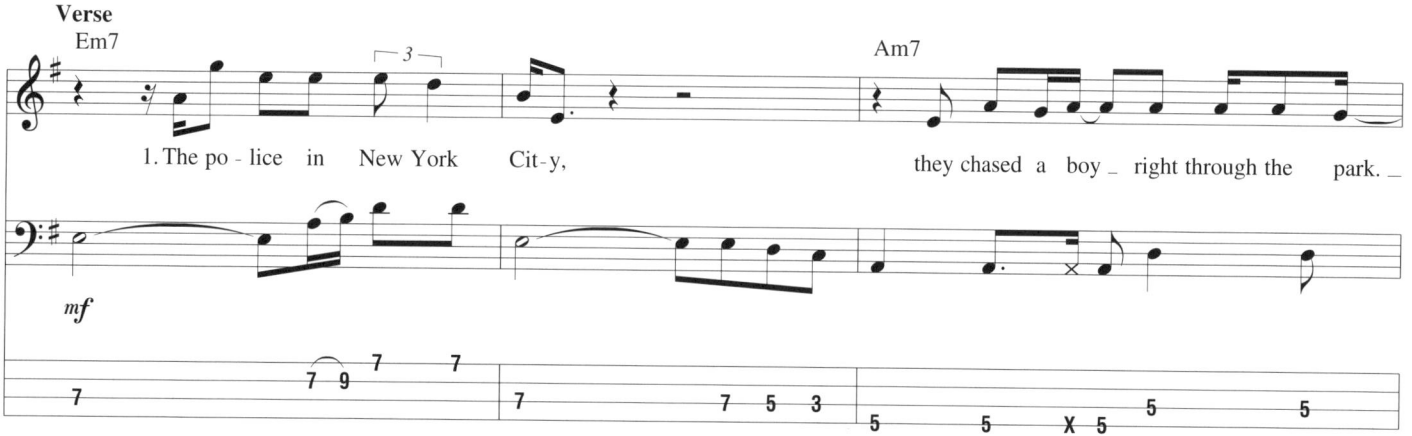

© 1973 EMI MUSIC PUBLISHING LTD.
All Rights for the U.S. and Canada Controlled and Administered by COLGEMS-EMI MUSIC INC.
All Rights Reserved   International Copyright Secured   Used by Permission

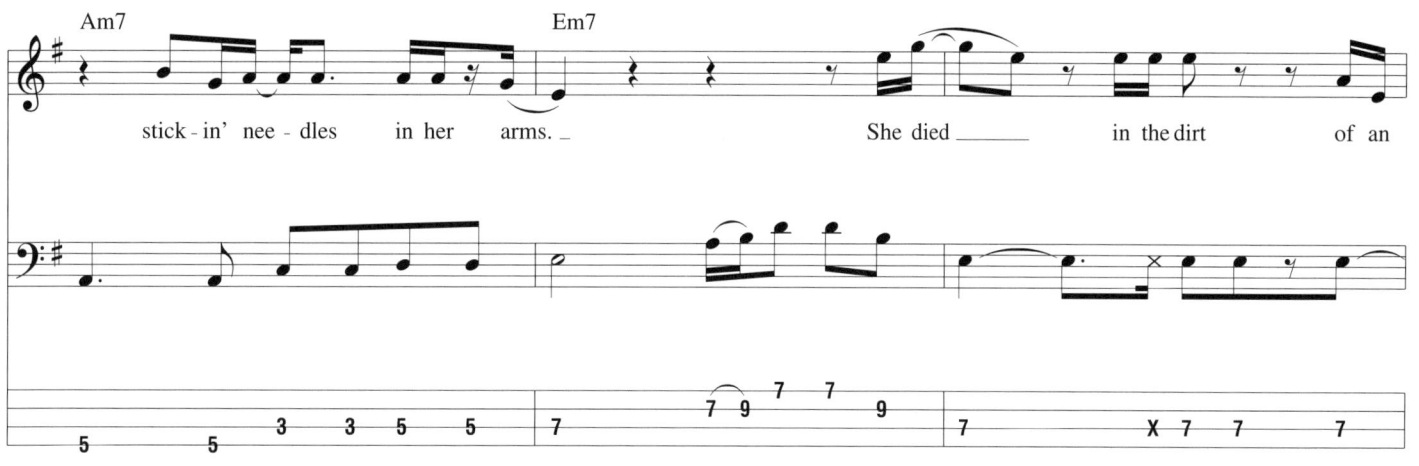

Chorus

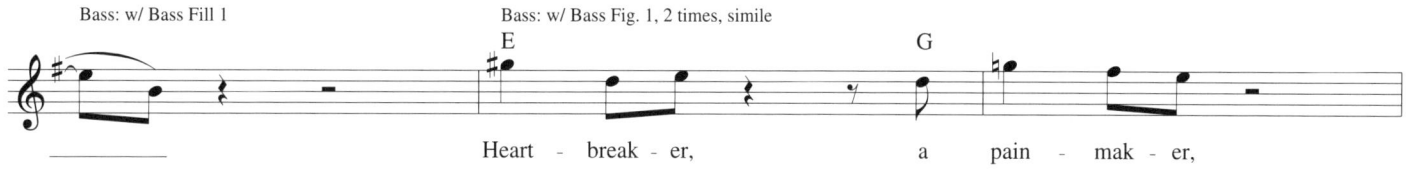

19

* Vocal doubled one octave lower, next 10 meas.

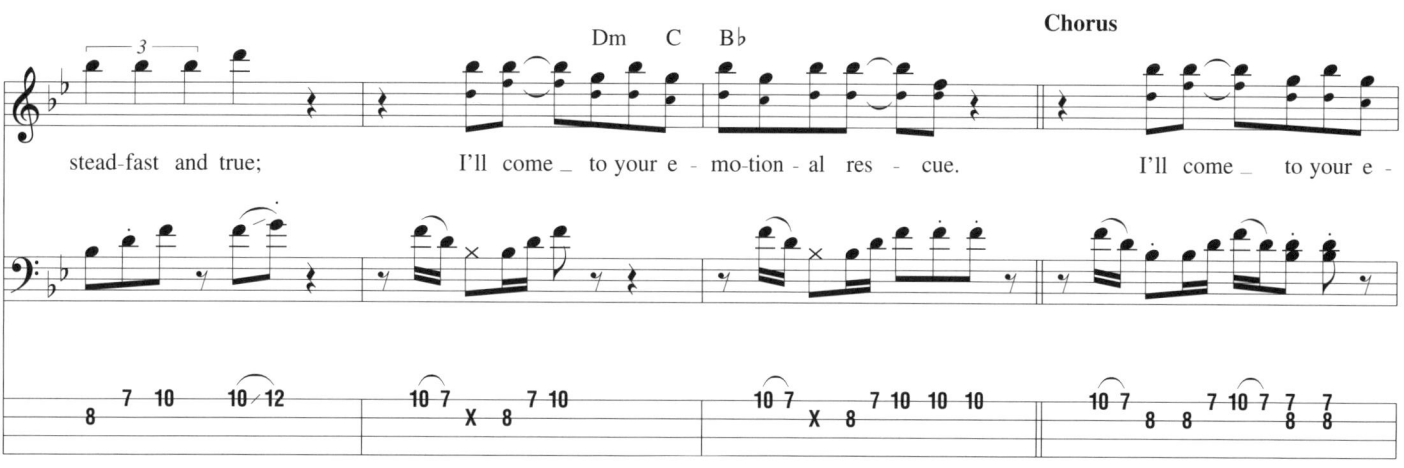

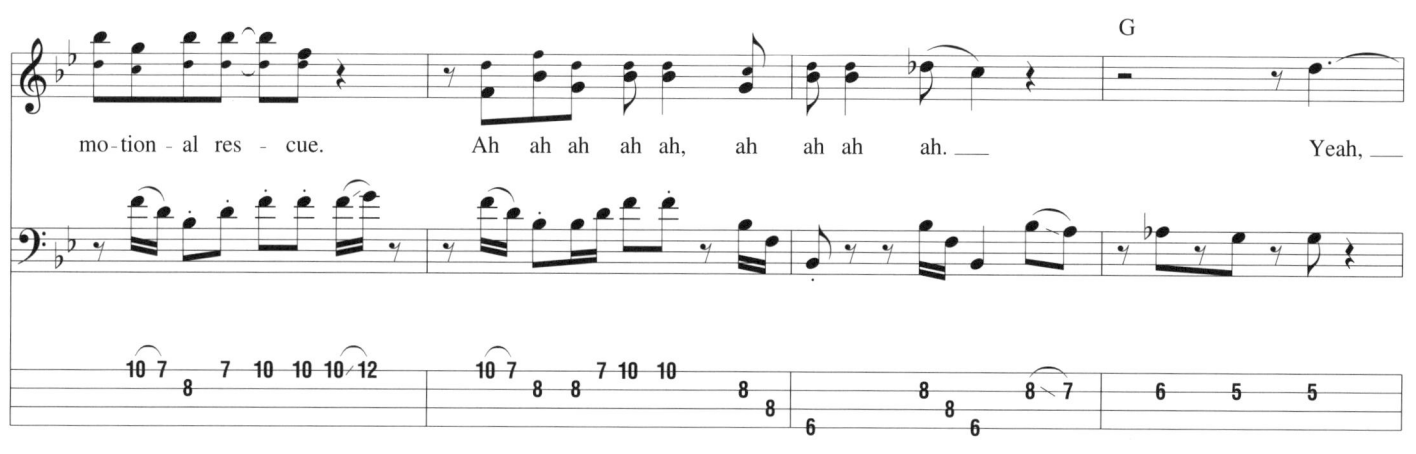

31

from *Tattoo You*
Hang Fire
Words and Music by Mick Jagger and Keith Richards

F♯m/C♯ D5 E5 A5
Hang fire, hang fire, hang fire.
doo doo doo doo, doo doo doo doo, doo doo doo doo. Doo doo doo doo,
F♯m D5 E5
Hang fire, hang fire. Put it all on the wire, ba - by.
doo doo doo doo, doo doo doo doo, doo doo doo doo.
A5 F♯m/C♯ D5 E
Yeah, take
Doo doo doo doo, doo doo doo doo, doo doo doo doo, doo doo doo doo.)
A5 F♯m/C♯ D5
a thou-sand dol - lars, go have some fun. Put it all on at a

E
A5
F♯m/C♯
D5
hun-dred to one. Hang fire. A-hang fire.
(Hang fire.)
E5
A5
F♯m
Throw it on the wire, ba - by. A - hang
(Doo doo doo doo, doo doo doo doo,
D5
E5
A5
fire, hang fire. Hang fire, hang fire, hang fire,
(On the wire, ba - by. Put it on the wire.)
doo doo doo doo, doo doo doo doo. Doo doo doo doo,
F♯m
D5
E5
Am
hang fire. Put it on the wire, ba-by. Put it on the wire.
doo doo doo doo, doo doo doo doo, doo doo doo doo.)

from *Dirty Work*

The Harlem Shuffle

Written by Robert Relf and Earl Nelson

40

by, (Yeah, come on ba - by.) don't fall down on me now. Just
A♭m
move it right here to the Har-lem Shuf - fle. (Woo.)
8va
Chorus
loco
Yeah, yeah, yeah, do the Har-lem Shuf - fle.
Yeah, yeah, yeah, do the Har-lem Shuf - fle.

Interlude

A7

A♭m ... *Am*

Verse

3. Hitch, hitch-hike ba - by, a - cross the floor.

Whoa, whoa, whoa, I can't stand it no more.

B♭7
Now, come on ba - by. Get in-to your slide. Just
(Yeah, come on ba-by now.)
Am
ride, ride, ride, lit-tle po - ny ride.
Chorus
Voc. Fig. 1
End Voc. Fig. 1
Yeah, yeah, yeah, do the Har-lem Shuf - fle. Woo.
Yeah, yeah, yeah, do the Har-lem Shuf - fle. (Do the mon-key shine.)

Yeah, yeah, yeah, shake a tail feath-er, ba - by. (Shake shake. Shake, shake.)
Yeah, yeah, yeah, shake a tail feath-er, ba - by. Woo.
Voc.:w/ Voc. Fig. 1, 4 times, simile
Begin Fade
Fade Out

from It's Only Rock 'N' Roll

It's Only Rock 'n' Roll (But I Like It)

Words and Music by Mick Jagger and Keith Richards

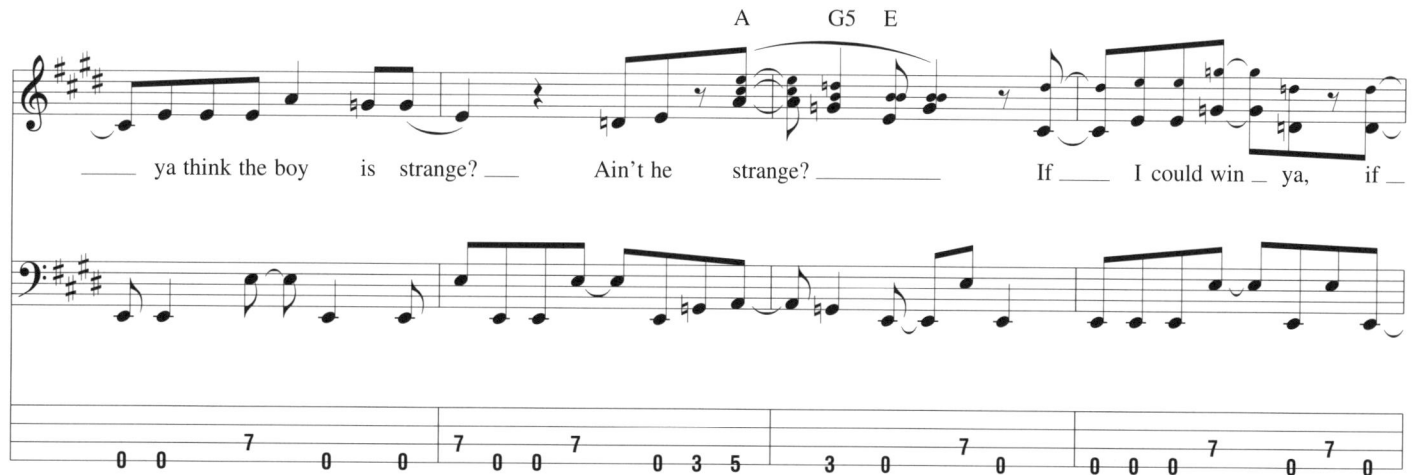

46

A E A E
yes, I do. Uh, well, I like it, uh. Oh! I like it.
A D A
I like it. I said, can't ya see that
D A E
this old boy has been a - lone - ly, uh. 2. If
Verse
E A G/A
I could stick a knife in my heart, su - i - cide right on the stage, would

48

E A5
on - ly rock 'n' roll, _ but I like it, _____ uh. I said, I know _ it's
E D A E A
on - ly rock 'n' roll, _ but I like it, like it, yes, I do, _ uh, well, I like it, uh.
E A
Yeah! _ I like it. I like it, _____ uh.
D A D A E
I said, can't ya see _ that this old boy _ has been a - lone - ly? _____

Bridge
B E/B B E/B B D/A A D/A
Mm. And do you think that you're the on - ly girl a - round?
A E/B B E/B B D/A A
Uh! I bet ya think that you're the on - ly wom-an in town,
C#5 F#5 A
Guitar Solo
uh! Oo! Yeah!
A G/A E A

Outro-Chorus
G5 E
A5
I said, I know it's only rock 'n' roll, but I
E
like it.
A5
I said, I know it's
E
only rock 'n' roll, but I like it, uh.
Whoo!
A5
I know it's
E
only rock 'n' roll, but I like it, uh.
Oo, yeah!
A5
I know it's

E D A E A5
on - ly rock 'n' roll, but I like it, like it, yes, I do. Uh, well, I like it,
mp
E A
I like it, uh. I like it, uh.
(Yeah, yeah.)
let ring
E A
(Inhale) I like it. I like it.
let ring
E A
I like it. ...I
(On - ly rock 'n' roll, but ...)
let ring

E
like it.
...I like it.
(On - ly rock 'n' roll, but ...)
(On -
grad cresc.
let ring
A
Oo, I like it.
- ly rock 'n' roll, but ...)
Oo, yeah! I
(On - ly rock 'n' roll, but ...)
E
like it.
Yeah! I
(On - ly rock 'n' roll, but ...)
A
like it.
(On -
mf
E
Oo, yeah! I like it.
- ly rock 'n' roll, but ...)
Oo, yeah! I
(On - ly rock 'n' roll, but ...)

A
E
like it.
Oo, yeah!
I like it.
(On - ly rock 'n' roll, but ...)
(On -
A
Oo, yeah!
I like it.
Oo, yeah.
I
- ly rock 'n' roll, but ...)
(On - ly rock 'n' roll, but ...)
E
A
like it.
Oh, but I like it.
uh.
(On - ly rock 'n' roll, but ...)
(On -
E
A
Oh, but I like it.
uh.
Yeah.
I
- ly rock 'n' roll, but ...)

E
like it.
Oo, but I like it.
And _ I said I
A
E
like it.
Oo, yeah, ______ I like it. __
Begin Fade
A
E
Fade Out
A
E

from *Some Girls*

Miss You

Words and Music by Mick Jagger and Keith Richards

Am
I've been hang-in' on _ the phone, _ I've been sleep-in' all _ a-lone. I wan-na
Dm7
Chorus
Am
kiss you some-time. Oo _ hoo _ oo, _ oo _ hoo _ oo, _ hoo _
Dm7
Am
oo oo, now. _ Oo _ hoo _ oo, _ oo _ hoo _ oo, _ oo _
Dm7
Verse
Am
oo oo, yah. _ 2. Well, I've been haunt - ed in _ my sleep, you been star -

Dm7
in' in my dreams. Lord, I miss you, child. I've been
(Spoken: Play it, Ron!)
Am
Dm7
wait-in' in the hall, been wait-in' on your call, when the phone rings. Spoken: It's just some friends
Am
of mine. They say, "Hey! What's the mat-ter man? We're gon-
Dm7
na come 'round at twelve with some Puer-to Ri-can girls that's just dy'n to

Am
meet you! We're gon - na bring a case of wine. Hey, let's go mess and fool a-round you know,
Dm7
like we used to!"
Chorus
Am
(Ah ah ah, ah ah ah, ah
Dm7
Am
I say, well... Ah
ah ah.)
(Ah ah ah, ah ah ah, ah
let ring
Dm7
Bridge
F
ah ah.
ah ah.)
Oh, oo, ba -
(Oo.

Em7
Dm7
by, why you wait so long
)
Yeah.
F
Em7
Dm7
Oh, ba - by, why you wait so long
(Oo.)
Won't ya
Interlude
E
N.C.(Am)
(Dm)
come home! Come home!
Spoken: Ahh...
T' t-'ck, t' t-'ck, t' t-'ck
(Spoken: Come home now, baby. Ya know what I'm sayin'...)
p
mp
(Am)
t' 'ck!
I've been walk - in' Cen - tral Park,
sing-in' af - ter dark.
Peo-ple think

(Dm)
(Am)
I'm cra - zy.
Stum-bl - in' on my feet,
shuff - lin' to the street.
(Dm)
Ask - in' me, "'Ch 'ch 'ch!
What's the mat-ter with you, boy?"
(Am)
(Dm)
Dm7
Some-time I wan-na say, to, to my-self...
Some-time I say...
Oo
Chorus
Am
Dm7
hoo oo, oo hoo oo, oo oo oo, yeah.
Oo
mf

62

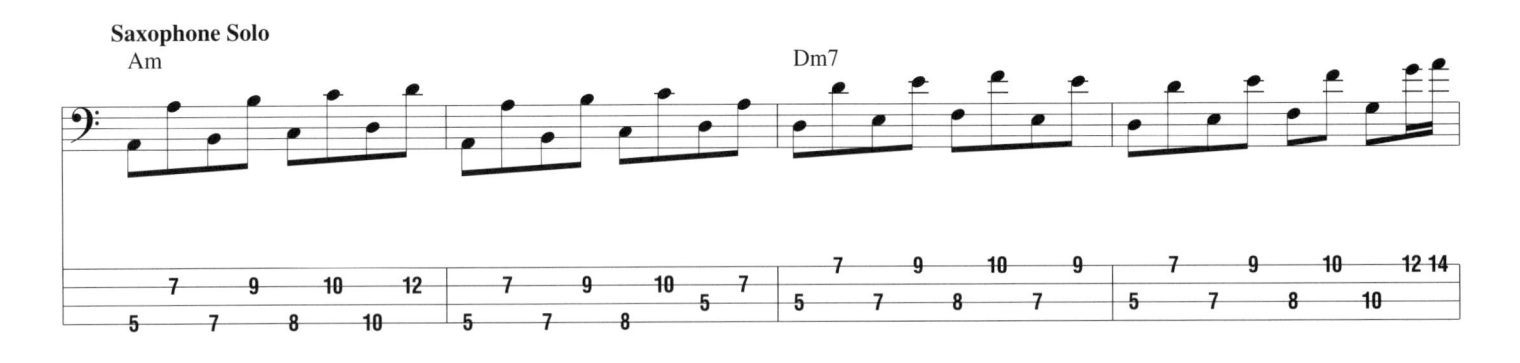

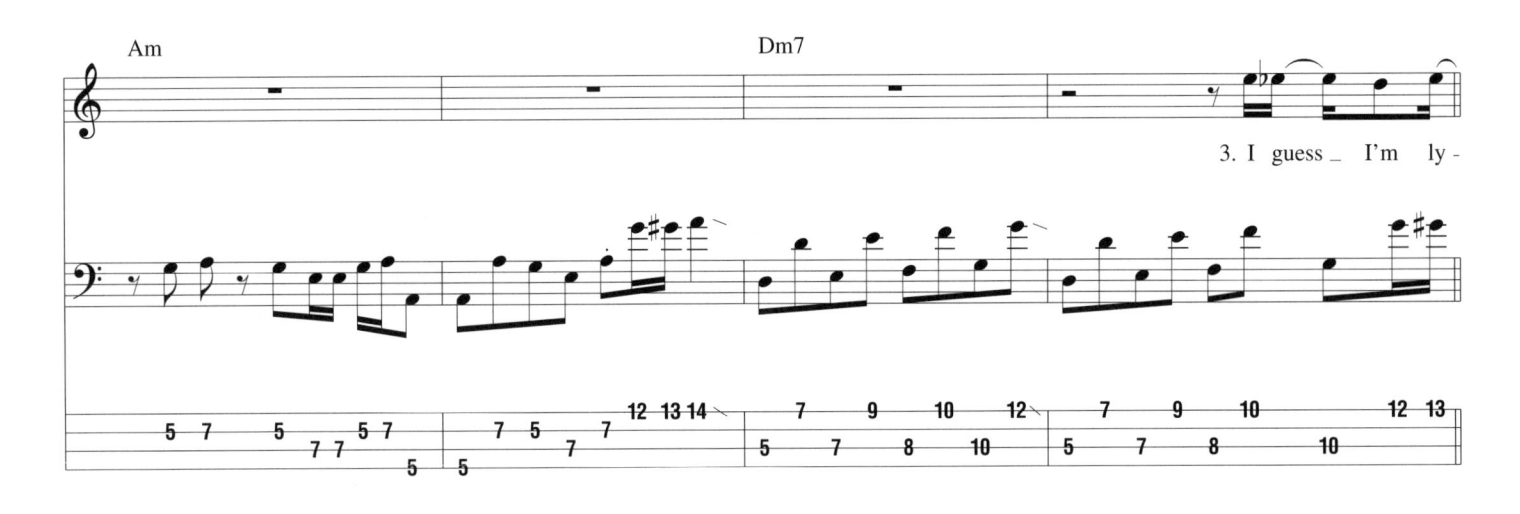

Am
Dm7
blot - tin'out _ my mind, _ fool-in'on _ my time. _ Lord, I wan-na kiss _ you, ba - by, _ yeah. ____ Lord, _
Am
Dm7
___ I miss you, child. ____ Oo, ____ hoo, __ ah, ______________ ah, ah, 'h!
(Ah _
Chorus
Am
Dm7
Uh, uh, uh! Huh, __________________ uh, _ uh! Lord, _ I miss you, child. _
ah __ ah, ____ ah __ ah __ ah, ________ ah _________ ah ah. __________) (Ah _
Am
Dm7
Lord, __ I miss you, child. _
ah ___ ah, ___ ah ___ ah ___ ah, ___ ah ___ ah ah. _________ (Ah ___

Am
Dm7
Oo oo oo, oo hoo oo. Come on, Dave, play it for me now!
ah ah, ah ah ah, ah ah ah.)
Harmonica Solo
Am
Dm7
Yeah!
Am
Dm7
Begin Fade
Am
Dm7
Am
Dm7
Fade Out

from *Some Girls*
Respectable
Words and Music by Mick Jagger and Keith Richards

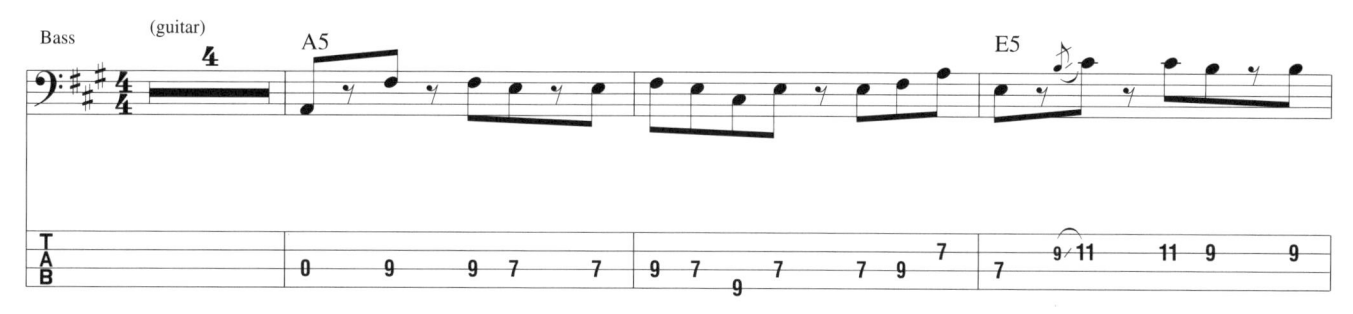

A5
Pres - i-dent. "Yes, there's a prob - lem, sir, __ but it can be bent," _ uh. Ah, yeah! __
End Bass Fig. 1
Verse
A5
2. Well, now __ you're a pil-lar of so -
D5
ci - e-ty. __ You don't wor - ry 'bout the things that used to be. You're a rag __ trade girl, _ you're the
A5
queen of porn. _ You're the ea - si - est lay __ on the White __ House lawn. _ Get out -

E5
A5
ta my life, _ don't come back. _ Get out-
E5
A5
ta my life _ don't come back! _ She's so re-
Chorus
A5
spect - a - ble. _ She's so re - spect - a - ble. _ She's so de-
D5
A5
lect - a - ble. _ She's so re - spect - a - ble. _ Get
(Get out-

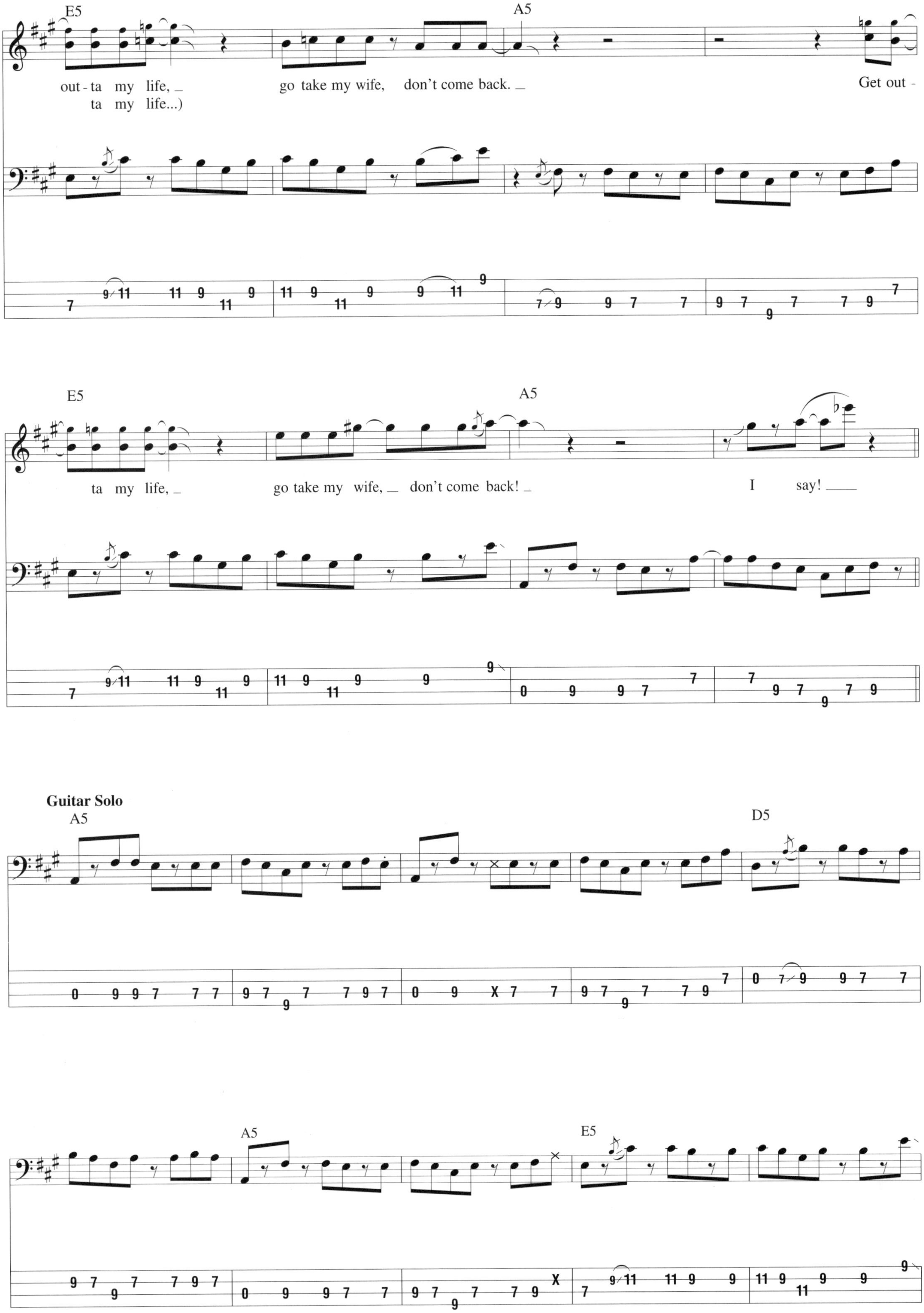
E5
A5
out - ta my life, _ go take my wife, don't come back. _ Get out -
ta my life...)
E5
A5
ta my life, _ go take my wife, _ don't come back! _ I say! ____
Guitar Solo
A5
D5
A5
E5

Chorus
A5
She's so re - spect - a - ble.
She's so re -
D5
spect - a - ble, huh. She's so re - spect - a - ble, huh. So re -
A5
E5
spect-a - ble.
(Tal - ly - ho!)
Get out - ta my life, go take my wife, don't come back!
A5
E5
A get out - ta my life, go take my wife, don't come back!

Guitar Solo
A5
All right, boys!
D5
A5
E5
A5
She's so re -
Chorus
Bass: w/ Bass Fig. 1, simile
A5
spect - a - ble.
She's so re - spect - a - ble.
She's so de -
D5
lect - a - ble.
A5
She's so re - spect - a - ble.
Get out -

-ta my life, go take my wife, don't come back! Whoo! Ah.

A get out-ta my life, go take my wife, don't come back!

Get out-ta my life, go take my wife, don't come back,

Free Time

come back! Ah!

rit.

71

from *Emotional Rescue*
She's So Cold
Words and Music by Mick Jagger and Keith Richards

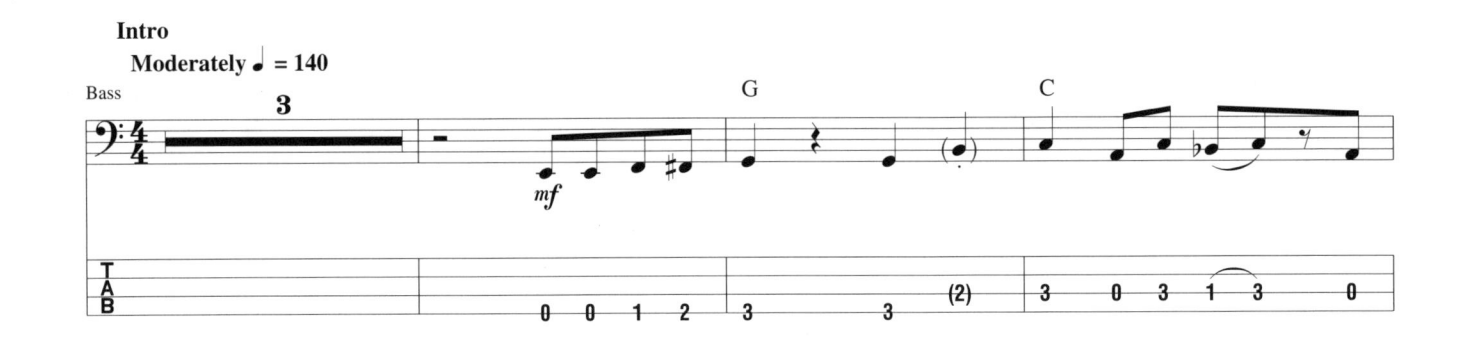

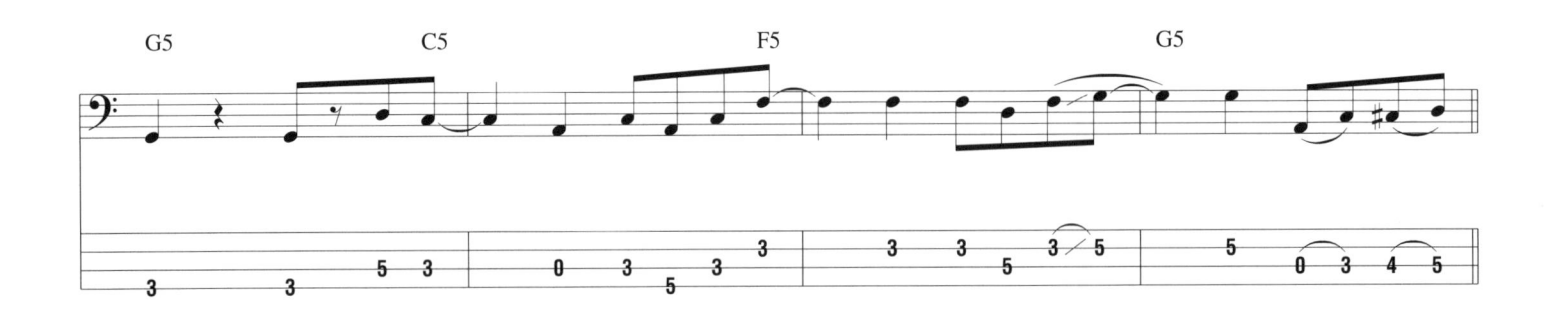

I'm the burn-in' bush, I'm the burn-in' fire, I'm the bleed-in' vol-ca-no. Well,

I'm so hot for her, I'm so hot for her, I'm so hot for her, she's so cold.

2. Yes, I

Verse

tried re-wir-in' her, tried re-fir-in' her, I think her en-gine is per-ma-nent-ly stalled. (So

Cadd9 F G
She's so cold, she's so cold, she's so cold, cold, cold, like a tomb - stone.
cold, so cold.)
Cadd9 F G
She's so cold, she's so cold, she's so cold, cold, cold, like an ice cream cone.
Cadd9 F G5
She's so cold, she's so cold, a - when I touch her my hand just froze.
C5 F5 G5
3. Yeah,

Verse
C F5 G5
I'm so hot for her, I'm so hot for her, I'm so hot for that queen of snow. _ Put your
(Put your
C5 F5 G5
hand on the heat, put your hand on the heat. A - come on, ba - by, let's go, go.
hand on the heat, put your hand on the heat. Come on, ba - by, let's go.
C5 F5 G
She's so cold, she's so cold, cold, _ she's so c - c - cold, but's she's beaut - i - ful, though.
She's so cold, she's so cold, cold, _ she's so c - c - cold, cold, but's she's beaut - i - ful, though.)
Cadd9 F G
Yeah! She's so cold!

76

hand just froze. She's so cold, she's so god-damn cold, she's so cold, cold, cold, she's so
(She's so cold.)

cold.

Verse

5. 'N' who will be-lieve you were a beau-ty in-deed when the

days get short-er and the nights get long? Light fades and the
(Light fades and the

(F) (G) (C)
rain comes; no - bod - y will know. When you're old, when you're
rain comes; no - bod - y will know. When you're old, when you're
steady gliss.
(F) (G) G Cadd9
old, no - bod - y will know that you was a beau-ty, a
old, no - bod - y will know.)
F G
sweet, sweet beau-ty, a sweet, sweet beau-ty, but stone stone cold! You're so cold, you're so
Cadd9 F G G5 C5
cold, cold, cold. You're so cold, you're so cold. I'm so hot for you,

I'm so hot for you, I'm so hot for you and you're so cold. I'm the burn-in' bush,

I'm the burn-in' fire, I'm the bleed-in' vol-ca-no.

from *Tattoo You*
Start Me Up
Words and Music by Mick Jagger and Keith Richards

F Fsus2 F Fsus2 G5 B♭5 F5 Fsus2
The job we're rig-gin' now don't blow my top. If you start me up, uh,
F Fsus2 F G5 B♭5
if you start me up, I'll nev-er stop, nev-er stop, nev-er stop, I'll nev-er stop.
Chorus
C5 D5 F5
You make a grown man
(You make a grown man
C5 D F E♭5 D5 D5 F5
cry. You make a grown man cry. You make a grown man
cry. You make a grown man cry. You make a grown man
E♭5 D5 C5 C6 C5 E♭5
cry. Spread out the oil, the gas-o-line. I want a smooth ride in a
cry.)

D5 C5 Fsus2 F Fsus2 F Fsus2 F B♭5
mean, mean ma - chine. Start it up.
B♭5
Verse
F5 Fsus2 F Fsus2 F Fsus2 B♭5
You can start me up. Kick on the start-er, give it all you've got, you've got,
(Start me up.)
F5 B♭5 F/A B♭5
you've got. I can com-pete with the rid-ers in the oth-er heats. If you
F5 B♭5
rough it up, 'n' if you like it, you can start it up, start it up, start it up, start it up.

Chorus
C5 D5 F5 E♭5 D5 C5 C D5 F5 E♭5 D5 C5
Don't make a grown man cry. Don't make a grown man cry.
(Don't make a grown man cry. Don't make a grown man cry.
D5 F5 E♭5 C Fadd9/C C Fadd9/C C
Don't make a grown man cry. My eyes di-late, my lips go green.
Don't make a grown man cry.)
E♭5 D5 E♭5 D5 C F/C C F/C C F/C
My hands are greas-y, she's a mean, mean ma-chine.
Verse
B♭5 B♭6 B♭5 B♭6 B♭5 B♭ E♭/B♭ B♭ C Fadd9/C C Fadd9/CF F/C
Start it up. 3. Mm, start me up. Now, give it

Bb5 Bb6 Bb5 Bb6 Bb5 Bb C F/C C
all you've got, you've got to nev - er, nev - er, nev - er stop. Start it up. Whoo!
F/C C5 F/C Bb5 Bb6 Bb5 Bb C5
Oh, baby, why don't ya start it up? Nev - er, nev - er, nev - er.
(Start it up. Start it up.)
Chorus
D5 F5 Eb5 C5 G F5
You make a grown man cry. You make a grown man
You make a grown man cry. You make a grown man
Eb5 C5 G5 F5 Eb5 D5 G
cry. You make a grown man cry.
cry. You make a grown man cry.)

C F/C C F/C C E♭ C
Ride like the wind at dou - ble speed. I'll take you plac - es that you
E♭5 D5 C5 F5 C/E F5 C/E F5 F/A B♭5
nev - er, nev - er seen.
B♭ E♭/B♭ B♭5 C5
Verse
F/C C Fadd9/C C F/C
3. Once you start it up, let me tell you, we will
B♭5 B♭6 B♭5 B♭ C5 F/C C Fadd9/C
nev - er stop, we'll nev - er stop, we'll nev - er, nev - er nev - er stop. Start me up.

Outro
C F/C B♭5 C5 C Fadd9/C C
We'll nev-er stop, nev-er stop. You, you,
F/C C F/C B♭ E♭/B♭ B♭ C F/C C
you made a grown man cry. You,
Begin Fade
F/C C F/C B♭ E♭/B♭ B♭ C F/C C
you made a dead man come. You, you,
Fade Out
F/C C F/C B♭5 B♭6 B♭5 B♭6 B♭ C Fadd9/C C
you made a dead man come. Yeah. And you, you,

from *Exile on Main St.*
Tumbling Dice
Words and Music by Mick Jagger and Keith Richards

Intro
Moderate Rock ♩ = 112
N.C.   B
(guitar)

Mm, _____ yeah. _____
(Woo! _____)

Bass
f

Verse
B

1. Wom-en think I'm tast-y, but they're al-ways try'n' to waste me, make

me burn the can-dle right down _____ but ba-by, ba-by, I

© 1972 EMI MUSIC PUBLISHING LTD.
All Rights for the U.S. and Canada Controlled and Administered by COLGEMS-EMI MUSIC INC.
All Rights Reserved   International Copyright Secured   Used by Permission

88

F♯ B F♯ B N.C.(E)
Ba - by, I can't stay. You got to roll me and
B
Verse
B
call me the tum - bl - in' dice. 4. Al - ways in a hur - ry. I
nev - er stop to wor - ry. Don't see the time flash - in' by.
F♯ B F♯ B E F♯ B
Hon - ey, got no mon - ey. I'm all six - es and sev - ens and nines. 5. Say

Verse
now, ba - by, I'm the rank out - sid - er. You can be my part - ner in crime.
F♯ B F♯ B
But ba - by, I can't stay. You got to
N.C.(E)
roll me and call me the tum - bl - in'... Roll me and
B
call me the tum - bl - in' dice.
Guitar Solo
B

91

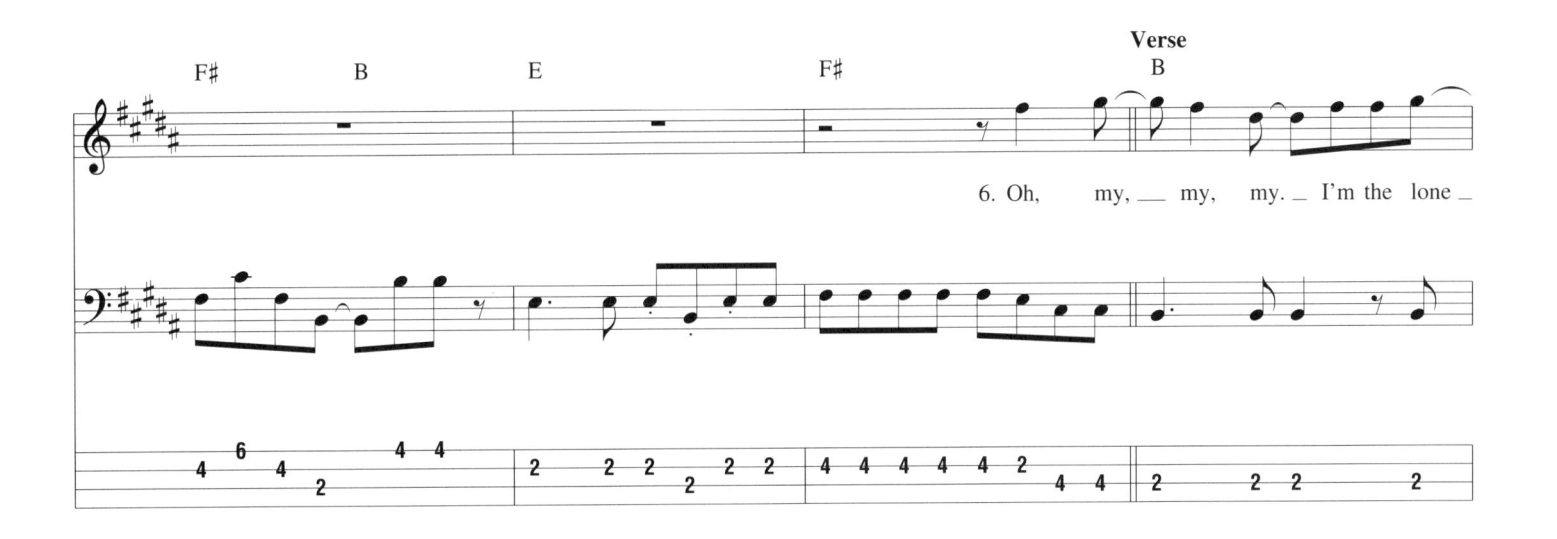

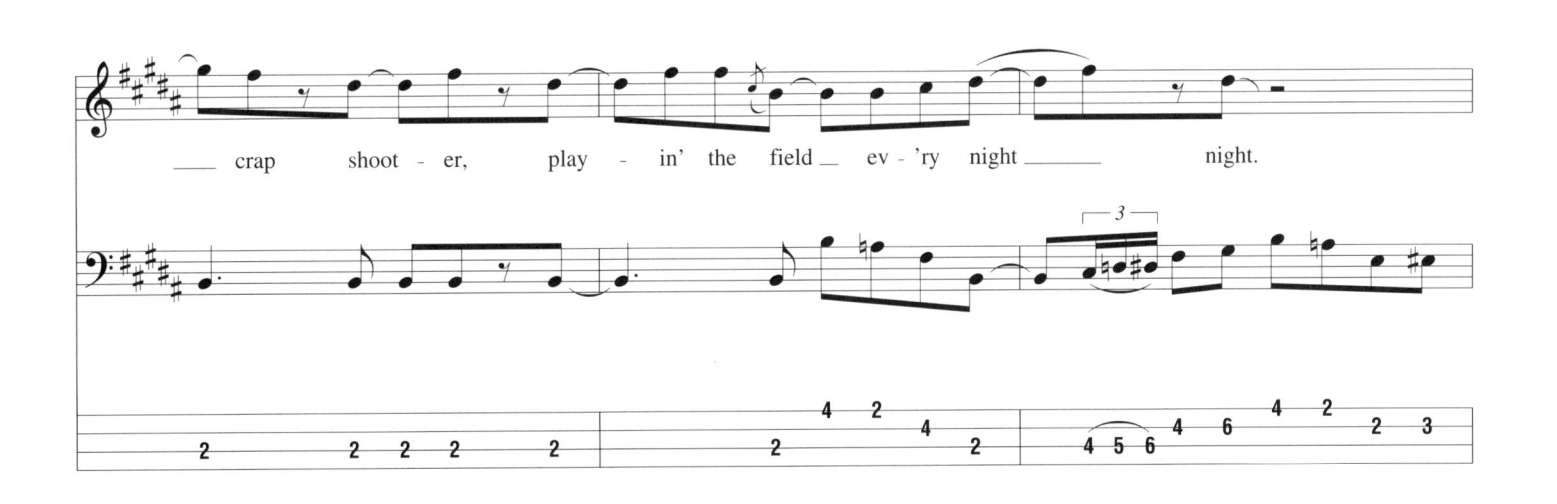

(B)
Roll me. Call me the tum - bl - in' dice.
(Dice.) (Got to roll me. Got to
(E) (B) (E) (B)
Oh, mm, yeah.
roll me. Got to roll me. Got to
(E) (B) (E) (B)
Ah, oh. Ah, yeah.
roll me. Got to roll me. Got to
(E) (B) (E) (B)
Keep on roll - in'. Keep on roll - in'.
roll me. Got to roll me. Got to

w/Lead Voc. ad lib., till end
(E) (B) N.C.(E) (B)
Keep on roll - in'.
roll me. Got to roll me. Got to
(E) (B) (E) (B)
roll me. Got to roll me. Got to
(E) (B) (E) (B)
roll me. Got to roll me. Got to
Repeat and Fade
(E) (B) (E) (B)
roll me. Got to roll me. Got to

Bass Notation Legend

Bass music can be notated two different ways: on a *musical staff*, and in *tablature*.

THE MUSICAL STAFF shows pitches and rhythms and is divided by bar lines into measures. Pitches are named after the first seven letters of the alphabet.

TABLATURE graphically represents the bass fingerboard. Each horizontal line represents a string, and each number represents a fret.

HAMMER-ON: Strike the first (lower) note with one finger, then sound the higher note (on the same string) with another finger by fretting it without picking.

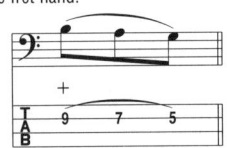

PULL-OFF: Place both fingers on the notes to be sounded. Strike the first note and without picking, pull the finger off to sound the second (lower) note.

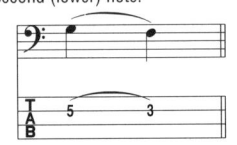

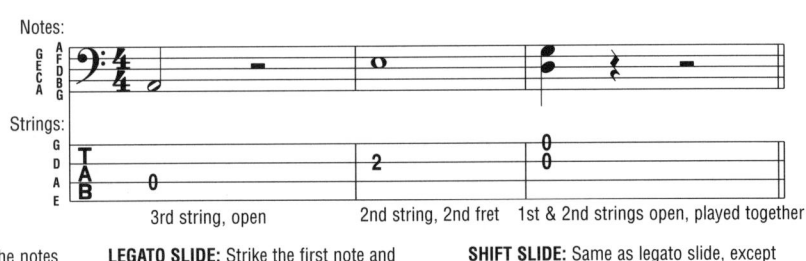

LEGATO SLIDE: Strike the first note and then slide the same fret-hand finger up or down to the second note. The second note is not struck.

SHIFT SLIDE: Same as legato slide, except the second note is struck.

TRILL: Very rapidly alternate between the notes indicated by continuously hammering on and pulling off.

TREMOLO PICKING: The note is picked as rapidly and continuously as possible.

VIBRATO: The string is vibrated by rapidly bending and releasing the note with the fretting hand.

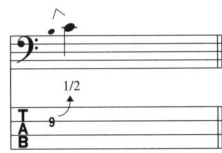

SHAKE: Using one finger, rapidly alternate between two notes on one string by sliding either a half-step above or below.

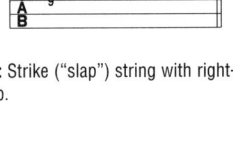

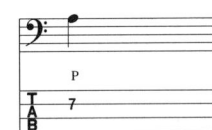

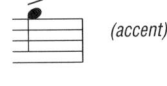

NATURAL HARMONIC: Strike the note while the fret hand lightly touches the string directly over the fret indicated.

MUFFLED STRINGS: A percussive sound is produced by laying the fret hand across the string(s) without depressing them and striking them with the pick hand.

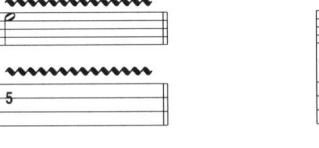

BEND: Strike the note and bend up the interval shown.

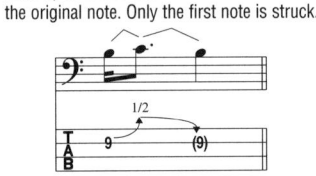

BEND AND RELEASE: Strike the note and bend up as indicated, then release back to the original note. Only the first note is struck.

RIGHT-HAND TAP: Hammer ("tap") the fret indicated with the "pick-hand" index or middle finger and pull off to the note fretted by the fret hand.

LEFT-HAND TAP: Hammer ("tap") the fret indicated with the "fret-hand" index or middle finger.

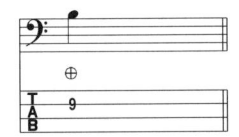

SLAP: Strike ("slap") string with right-hand thumb.

POP: Snap ("pop") string with right-hand index or middle finger.

Additional Musical Definitions

(accent)	Accentuate note (play it louder)	***D.C. al Fine***	Go back to the beginning of the song and play until the measure marked "***Fine***" (end).
(accent)	Accentuate note with great intensity	**Bass Fig.**	Label used to recall a recurring pattern.
(staccato)	Play the note short	**Fill**	Label used to identify a brief pattern which is to be inserted into the arrangement.
⊓	Downstroke	tacet	Instrument is silent (drops out).
V	Upstroke		Repeat measures between signs.
D.S. al Coda	Go back to the sign (𝄋), then play until the measure marked "***To Coda***," then skip to the section labelled "***Coda***."	1. 2.	When a repeated section has different endings, play the first ending only the first time and the second ending only the second time.

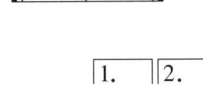

NOTE: Tablature numbers in parentheses mean:
1. The note is being sustained over a system (note in standard notation is tied), or
2. The note is sustained, but a new articulation (such as a hammer-on, pull-off, slide or vibrato begins, or
3. The note is a barely audible "ghost" note (note in standard notation is also in parentheses).

94

BASS RECORDED VERSIONS

Recorded Versions for Bass Guitar are straight off-the-record transcriptions done expressly for bass guitar. This series features the best in bass licks from the classics to contemporary superstars. Also available are Recorded Versions for Guitar, Easy Recorded Versions and Drum Recorded Versions. Every book includes notes and tab.

Beatles Bass Book
00660103 / $14.95

Best Bass Rock Hits
00694803 / $12.95

Black Sabbath – We Sold Our Soul For Rock 'N' Roll
00660116 / $14.95

The Best Of Eric Clapton
00660187 / $14.95

Stuart Hamm Bass Book
00694823 / $19.95

The Buddy Holly Bass Book
00660132 / $12.95

Best Of Kiss
00690080 / $19.95

Lynyrd Skynyrd Bass Book
00660121 / $14.95

Michael Manring – Thonk
00694924 / $22.95

Alanis Morisette – Jagged Little Pill
00120113 / $14.95

Nirvana Bass Collection
00690066 / $17.95

Pearl Jam – Ten
00694882 / $14.95

Pink Floyd – Dark Side Of The Moon
00660172 / $14.95

Pink Floyd – Early Classics
00660119 / $14.95

The Best Of The Police
00660207 / $14.95

Queen – The Bass Collection
00690065 / $17.95

Rage Against the Machine
00690248 / $14.95

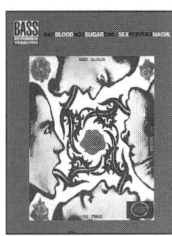

Red Hot Chili Peppers – Blood Sugar Sex Magik
00690064 / $17.95

Red Hot Chili Peppers – One Hot Minute
00690091 / $18.95

Best Of U2
00694783 / $18.95

Stevie Ray Vaughan – In Step
00694777 / $14.95

Stevie Ray Vaughan – Lightnin' Blues 1983-1987
00694778 / $19.95

FOR MORE INFORMATION, SEE YOUR LOCAL MUSIC DEALER, OR WRITE TO:

HAL•LEONARD® CORPORATION
7777 W. BLUEMOUND RD. P.O. BOX 13819 MILWAUKEE, WI 53213

Prices, contents & availability subject to change without notice.